T0273500

SNAKE:

ORIGINAL GRACE

Snake:
Original Grace

BOOK IV

of

Snake Quartet

Gary Lemons

RED HEN PRESS | PASADENA, CA

Snake: Original Grace
Copyright © 2021 by Gary Lemons
All Rights Reserved

No part of this book may be used or reproduced in any manner whatsoever without the
prior written permission of both the publisher and the copyright owner.

Book layout by Mark E. Cull

Library of Congress Cataloging-in-Publication Data

Names: Lemons, Gary, author.
Title: Snake : original grace / Gary Lemons.
Description: Pasadena, CA : Red Hen Press, [2021] | Series: Snake quartet ; book 4
Identifiers: LCCN 2020044868 (print) | LCCN 2020044869 (ebook) | ISBN
    9781597091152 (trade paper) | ISBN 9781597098793 (epub)
Subjects: LCGFT: Poetry.
Classification: LCC PS3612.E475 S62 2021 (print) | LCC PS3612.E475
    (ebook) | DDC 811/.6—dc23
LC record available at https://lccn.loc.gov/2020044868
LC ebook record available at https://lccn.loc.gov/2020044869

The National Endowment for the Arts, the Los Angeles County Arts Commission, the
Ahmanson Foundation, the Dwight Stuart Youth Fund, the Max Factor Family Foun-
dation, the Pasadena Tournament of Roses Foundation, the Pasadena Arts & Culture
Commission and the City of Pasadena Cultural Affairs Division, the City of Los Angeles
Department of Cultural Affairs, the Audrey & Sydney Irmas Charitable Foundation, the
Kinder Morgan Foundation, the Meta & George Rosenberg Foundation, the Albert and
Elaine Borchard Foundation, the Adams Family Foundation, the Riordan Foundation,
Amazon Literary Partnership, the Sam Francis Foundation, and the Mara W. Breech
Foundation partially support Red Hen Press.

First Edition
Published by Red Hen Press
www.redhen.org

for Nöle

the whole frequency

Contents

Chorus

Chorus

Chorus

Chorus

Preface

In this last book in the *Snake Quartet* the first-person narrative dissolves at times into variations of the collective voices inside of snake—other witnesses—rare in the first three books—appear more frequently in this one. Snake is at the end of her journey through destruction into creation both as a blooded instrument and a myth. The bound voices sequestered in her for millions of years begin to speak in the poems. She is dying into life. Again.

There are essentially two themes in this final book.

The title poem—"Original Grace"—questions the endgame philosophy that says humans are born into sin and only by accepting and surrendering to gods and their proxies might they be saved on earth prior to an eternity in some variant of a place called heaven. Those who don't subscribe fully are eternally remaindered.

The doctrine of Original Sin is embedded in every child born to Christian families. Snake, before collapsing into metaphor, was human and as such, raised to believe she was impoverished and morally defective in the cradle. As the planet froze and burned and leapt and bucked its way into emptiness, she understood this to be revenge on a global scale for a system inhabited mostly by craven individuals incapable of finding true north without a borrowed compass no one understood was broken until they were lost.

When snake was a child in Sunday school in a Baptist church, she asked the teacher if it was true a baby that died at or soon after birth could be damned eternally. The teacher confirmed that without the intercession of a minister or priest the child was born condemned to Hell. Same with people from other cultures with different Gods and same with people without Gods—all damned either because they had not accepted a savior they'd never heard of or been baptized in his name. A little girl beside me started crying—she said—that's not fair. Snake never forgot her words.

So this book starts with the premise that we are born in a state of Grace and have to consciously choose to be evil—to kill—to abuse—to suppress—to be cruel—to deny others their rights. How we choose to live defines us and not some preexisting state of wickedness.

The *"him"* in the title poem "Original Grace" refers to a Sunday school song with the lines " little ones to him belong / they are weak but he is strong . . ."

The second dominant theme in the fourth book has to do with systems formed around the belief in Original Sin—particularly governmental but also societal and cultural mechanics founded on the principle we need to be saved from ourselves.

Systems composed of people weakened by doctrines informing them they are unworthy without the support and control of that system becomes quickly claustrophobic and hierarchal—just before they destroy themselves like an autoimmune disease attacking the body of its host.

Those who author these systems love the power and wealth that comes to them—they have unlimited access to resources and live in increasingly more insulated communities from those suffering under it. While white bears are starving on shrinking ice floes—while the last of a species is hunted for its horn—while the tropics burn and sand creeps out of the hourglass into the streets, they fiddle with their thermostats.

What would a different system look like? One designed to elevate its individual members in order to make a strong village—city—nation? A system with filters assuring equal distribution of wealth so no one has significantly more than anyone else. A system like this must surely be stronger—healthier—more durable—consequently more advanced—more equitable and more compassionate than the cages around us now. The opening line of the poem "Leadership" sums up snake's take on this—

If everyone has enough then

Everyone would have enough—

Pipe dream—bogus—impossible—only those closing the doors of their towers as the sea washes the foundation away will even question the fact that something needs to happen now. It is insufficient to supply Nero with rosin for his bow. And it will take the clearest minds—the most undisciplined visionaries—the most ferocious efforts as well as

The heaviest of hearts—the lightest of steps—the death of the dinosaurs—again—and the best collaborative spirit we can bring on behalf of the planet and those who will stand on the ground we prepare for them.

Gary Lemons
June 27, 2020

Author's Note

Stendahl said a novel is a mirror dragged down the road. I take the liberty to believe poetry shares with all art the responsibility and privilege to extract and hold up for witness the images—no matter how uplifting or despicable—found in the mirror of its time.

Snake wanders in these images—witnessing as well as participating in the catastrophic changes in climate—the loss of biodiversity and the suffering of animals— the acceleration of violence both personal and global and the endless sophistication of instruments intended to make numbness bearable.

The poems are also those of the witness. They are the poems of the child as it was told the names of things—as it was injured or loved or both at the same time— as it remembers against this collective backdrop the time when it and the world were without comparisons and new to the day.

The *Snake Quartet* is for that child and the ones to come—who will know by what we leave them how truly alone or accompanied they are.

SNAKE:

ORIGINAL GRACE

We may well be leaving to coming generations debris, desolation and filth. The pace of consumption, waste and environmental change has so stretched the planet's capacity that our contemporary lifestyle, unsustainable as it is, can only precipitate catastrophes.
—Pope Francis

We have not taken to the streets for you to take selfies with us, and tell us that you really admire what we do. We children are doing this to wake the adults up. We children are doing this for you to put your differences aside and start acting as you would in a crisis. We children are doing this because we want our hopes and dreams back.
—Greta Thunberg

Chorus

Snake remembers a time when
The aspiration of light flowed like blood
In a vein connecting different worlds

Where survivors stumbled between
Walled-off communities while some folks
Hid in towers burning books to keep warm—
Learning to live without substance
In the ghost towns of themselves.

Snake is fluid in an ocean of falling
Light incidentally filled with the discarded
And forlorn pieces the darkness
Leaves behind it like broken skies
In a wet spot that once was snow.

Maybe this don't mean much
To the besotted blowers of the fume
Suckling the furnace flame

But it means everything to those about
To stand up from the ruins—
Shake the ash from their hair—
And occupy the days to come.

Aesop

The fox watches everything.
It never blinks—seeing objects in the dark
As well as lifeguards see distant
Swimmers in a bright yellow glare
Pulled out to sea—the fox
Revolves her head when a single
Leaf crashes to earth—bang!

She's tuned into her world—
Alive as an exposed nerve
Touched at the same time
By different temperatures
Waiting for the world
To go dark so the paw in the trap
Will freeze before freedom
Requires it be left behind.

No one knows the fox is caught
In a snare left behind centuries ago
Except poets who imagines this—who
Like iron and blood—will never
Let go of the cold fire stolen
From her beautiful eyes.

The Conscript

1

Snake was born—in a ditch
Or a mansion or near kerosene
Soaked rags smoking in a fire
Beside a shepherd's hut—
She remembers the blood

Pulled through her body on thin wires
Attached to a spool in the hands
Of an angel longing to be flogged—
To feel something for the first time—
To moan ecstatically inside yellow
Flowers at dawn—to bloom from the verdant
Soil at the end of myth and die
In a cloud of drifting pollen.

Who hasn't undressed
Among strangers—who hasn't
Lain in the arms of death
Only to awaken unexpectedly
Perched on a moss-covered
Sundial watching the hours
Erased by the moon.

2
Snake was drunk when the ocean
Turned boardwalks into splinters
Re-used to frame wanted posters
Where the faces of the innocent slowly
Dissolved into the guilty as
The water rose and the ammo ran out—

She remembers the smell
Of cordite in her braids while shaving
A sister's legs with a bayonet in preparation
For lifting the great weight of brotherhood—

Her mind is on a blue hand
Back home—placing wild marigolds
In an old vase that belonged
To her mother and grandmother
When the family lived in one
Room along the banks of a river
So sad its tears kept the fish wet
Through the endless dry season.

The barracks are cramped and stink.
Smoke drifts between openings. Snake licks
The heavy pistol in her sister's hand
To taste yesterday's war.

3
Yet there are times perhaps
In a garden or beside a river or unbuttoning
A blouse when we look up to see
Giants falling from the sky who
Struggle through clouds to land
With a dusty thump among
Us—not to frighten even a small
Horse but simply to smell
The heather in bloom—the pink
Ones—the color of the blood lost
Inside memories.

4
Snake hates the point of anything—
Can't stand to be prodded—will
Go where she wants when she wants
And won't be forced into the service
Of a country whose victory marches
Start with men lighting firecrackers in
Their underwear while I hate to say—

Dogs are eaten by children
Hiding in the forests not yet burned
Down by inflammatory rhetoric
From chieftains who lie as easily
As they expectorate a coin—
Meaning anyone in service to the new flag
Is a partial citizen of despair and the moral
Equivalent of honey quivering
Inside a burning tree.

Ah the river where I was born
Says the conscript out loud as her
Sister's leg falls off the table leaving
Blood tracks on stark ribs like the spoor
Of a wolf that took the bait
With the bone inside.

War hatches out of peace
As unexpectedly as a sudden
Storm scatters petals of purple lupines
Growing from a slide at the bottom of a mountain

Where the cross of a crushed
Church lifts above the purple flowers
Into the purple light of sunset
Through which crows fly off
With rapture in their claws.

5

Snake is still dodging the magnums
Chilled by speeches hurled at new recruits
Draped in bloodshed fresh out of school—
She takes the bayonet after the last
Shaving stroke and begins the cut—
Her sister moans then reaches up
To touch snake's tail as the long
Day ends in a gush of lost hours.

Someone is reciting from the manual
Of malignant ignorance that duty is no more
Than poking out both eyes before
Humping carnivorous flowers
Between stockyard doors.

Her sister sings a lullaby
In the pre-Babel language of raptors
To the child she left behind.

6

The woman in the violet dress
Stretches her hands through the shrubs
To reach the blue eggs in the cone
Of bark and feathers but remembers
In time the world is not for touching
And so returns to her violin
To play a small air by Scarlatti
She adapted from the piano

By imagining herself as a broken
Tusk on a pachyderm pulling leaves
From an Acacia while trumpeting
To its mother in a distant zoo—

Not quite but close enough
To capture the hours and diligence
It takes to make a string and a bow
And rosin into food for a pulsing
Vein in a slender wrist

Or more precisely to arrange
Anything after a life of unexpected
Crescendos in such a way as to help
A small bird inside a blue
Egg fly into in the same world

Where music is the branch
On the tree where it lands.

7

The bugle is not content
To hang quietly in the hands
Of someone hoping to grow old
Nor is the drum ready to surrender its joy
To the fragments of a horse
Beside a wagon wheel

But the violin is always ready to celebrate
Any movement—holding still while
Releasing the light inside a tourniquet—

So the bugler and the drummer
Are the only ones to stop snapping
Each other in the shower with wet
Towels and go back to the uniforms
Laid out on their cots and prepare
Themselves for resurrection.

Snake is aware the enemy has snuck
Inside the enemy and is helping
Each soldier hum in the familiar
Key of a sadhu cooking food
In the palm of his hand.

Which is exactly what happens
When the paths in all directions—
The probabilities destroyed by faith
Then rebuilt from disbelief—

Roll her into a single speck
Of bright light within which every
Living fire refuses to go out even
As she crawls through ruins

Waving a black flag toward a setting sun
With a smoking ghoul on her back.

8

Snake was conscripted at birth
Into a girl or a boy or maybe
A nematode or bird—she don't remember
What hardened the paths around

Her only the room where strangers
Extracted her head with forceps
While doctors whispered as if too
Much noise might ignite an invisible
Fuse causing her to explode

Leaving no trace other than wildflowers
Beneath a crescent moon.

9

The poem too is a weight that must
Be carried—snake remembers lifting
Her sister's leg from the dirt floor—

How it was heavier than all the ideas
Or stories in the brimming books
In the libraries of the world—no
Lever or engine—no breakthrough
In engineering would ever move
That small discarded leg even one bit
From her memory and so it is not

Without recognition of the poor
Reliance vision provides that snake
Sees the conscript shaving the beard
Of the patriarch when the razor slips
And like a shark sucked from deep ocean then
Dropped by thunder into a poppy field
Something bright red blooms
In the rictus of her smile—

This is the poet waiting
For the poem to let go its
Need to make sense or assist
Morticians as they beautify the dead—
This is the poet free from poetry
Leading two horses across staked

Plains to drink from a mirage
While above them the sky fills
With parachutes beneath which
The legs of beautiful dancers
Dance as they fall.

10

The men are armatures
Wired together by acts of violence
Both physical and emotional
So grotesque even the mauve roses
In the wallpaper stop offering their beauty
To the gods of household light—

The men roam the cities breaking
Windows with the legs snapped off couches
Where homeless persons sleep—
Absorbing into their souls the sound
Of children rearranged by falling glass—

Snuffing candles and pulling
Manikins behind them because
When no one is available brutality
Still requires practice.

They are coming for your sons
And your daughters and they will
Saddle them green and bucking
Then ride them away tame.

We may cry for a million years
Then refill our canteen with sorrow's rain
But our thirst remains.

11
The question is who survives—
Is snake the summary of an endless night
Or the institution from which the unblinking eye
Looks out at even this brief comfort
From frozen memories at a teaspoon of rain
Carried between poets in gardens
Where nothing yet speaks.

Where family was a very old
Hand holding a match to a blackened wick
And all the faces stayed in shadow
When the tiny flame came—

Where the flood was a stranger
With one bullet left stalking a season
Far away but certain to arrive.

And my sister—
As the snow reddens beneath us—
Trembling in my arms—
Says—we've come a long way
Haven't we—

And I say yes—a long way—
So sleep awhile—we're almost there.

Bebop Baby

Snake slithers between cerebral
Fences not yet full erected to keep
Mastodons out of bubbling tar—she finds the place
Where Charlie Parker started it and fish
Cooked in it—where Romeo pulled his
Pants down and the Lionheart in tiny
Armor died beneath a lancer's charge—

She was there when it went down—
Her last throw of the dice across the fields
Of brown dirt came up snake eyes—

She holds her tail up in a tight
Loop so wind through the opening
Makes a sound like two violas
Thrown from a stage coach to lighten
The music a cello covets—

A sound like the clopping of velvet
Boots worn by lesser squires near a pavilion
Where ladies in waiting curtsey
To lords with codpieces imperfectly
Adjusted—the resultant wincing
Passing for aristocratic disdain—

Snake loves the silence
But digs the music from her tail
Even more—changing the size
Of the opening—running through
The scales—high on her bebop—

She's dancing toward the sunset—
Keeping time with the rhyme—the size
Of the prize at the end of the demise—

Got the last blackbird tucked
Away in her horn ready to come out
When the drummer makes a tree.

DEMIMONDE

Sometimes snake awakens
Walking in mountains or on city streets
Or astride a horse or pushed on playgrounds
Or in markets beside upturned
Stalls holding someone's hand.

She might dream of love
While looking into a still pool
Of deep water where a face
Looks back and it's all the day
Can do to keep us apart.

Awakening tunes the senses—tunes
Taste into seeing then the smell
Of sirens in a bloody glove—

Then she smells old scars where
The earth turns protein into flowers—
She hears the echo of questions from
Earlier times—now—the feel

Of that small hand in hers—the
Thorn beneath the rose all night—
The rushing sound of petals falling—
Swans landing everywhere.

How It Was

Snake watches the patriarchs
Of the free world pecking in the barnyard—

Sees them finish for the day
Then crawl through a knothole
Where they pull the curtains in an oval
Room inside a crumbling house

Before tethering their donkey to
Each other's light—oh what a sight—
Streaming cigar smoke

From open sores while floating like fish
Atop a moonlight reservoir.

The cigars set off smoke alarms
Whose shrieks make the fly strips
Shudder as if the snow leopards
Stuck to them still live.

Then the curtains can't be
Raised. The patriarchs strain
Even the thumb and finger that counts
Money or pinches a thigh but still
The ambient light is insufficient
To illuminate the exit doors
So they panic into one another's arms—

Where they continued to copulate
On the bed they made.

Longevity

Snake be old—no—that
Ain't right—snake's too old to be
Old—old got a feelin of time passin
And time done stopped far
As snake's concerned.

She don't need to run away
Or hide in dreams—she crawled a billion
Years past old Mr. Death busy
Silencing immobile instruments—

She watches death limp away
Into attending silhouettes—wipin'
Wet hands on its red apron—in the air
Above holes in the ground doves
Carry messages of permanence
Between the conquered tongues—

Death says—I'm so sorry snake—

I never meant to hurt them peoples—

I just wanted to stop them
From hurting themselves.

SNAKE AT THE DOOR

Snake gathers the dust
Then pours it in her ears—
Swallows it—packs it in her eyes—
Until the fictions burned out of the
Screams beneath daily acts of devotion
Begin to tell their story—

Sometimes the strongest grip
On the next moment comes
Upon things jettisoned to survive.

There's the squeal of wooden
Wheels hooped with bronze
Turning a corner in the arena
As men in armor stick one another
With tridents—whinnying horses maddened
By lion—this dust in the air today—
The trill of martial music—nocturnal
Emissions on a sharpened blade—

Snake listens—the last to leave
After the concert ends—straining
To hear the gravel voice of the husband
Coming out of the urn on the mantle—
Echoes of stars in the night sky—

Then the murmur of his wife—
The wheels of the chariot glinting—
The lazy-boy fully reclined—
The corn chips in crumbs

On the rug—the crowd demanding blood—
The lion guarding libraries—

She breaks the urn—vacuums his ashes
Then leaves the bag on the mantle
On her way into another life—

Though once in a while
She drinks the melted ice
From the drip of frozen
Dreams then opens her
Blue lips to spit out bones.

Echo

In houses and tunnels and towers—
Inside the minds of big operators—the power
Cords shorted out while transformers
Sparkled like dolphins in blue flowers—

Something awakens out of darkness
Confirming it is a bridge between mortals
The gods of dirty laundry cannot cross.

Maybe it was the last bee
Flying in descending circles toward
The mouth of someone spitting
Honey on a brush to paint over the
Face of a woman encircled by men
That broke her with stones.

What if her body is a gathering
Of strangers exchanging magnets
In a field of metal fragments impermanently
Released from a retrograde attraction
To a long extinguished light.

There no way to know who is
Running away or coming closer—

The one body doesn't mourn itself—
Unfolding as it is outside the hourglass—
Released from particulate attraction
To a long extinguished light—

No way to say who lived or died
From the things we didn't do.

Karma

Snake ain't no shaman—don't
Have a clue which quark be pointin
Its derrière out the porthole of a sneer—

Got a fancy hat and gold knob
On her cane—shuffling through
The dance as the floor underneath
Turns to water made red by the
Lipstick of the drowned.

Meanwhile in the tenement
Of an overly populated afterlife

A goddess stands on a chair shouting
At this serpent coming in through
The cat door to please stop chewing
The little mouse on the white carpet in
Such a manner the blood stains
Resemble embroidered roses.

Snake says—okay—I'll stop—
If you'll come down from that chair.

ABSENCE

Snake remembers a little girl
Becoming a teenager—the burst of speed
Through razors in mid-air—the clarity
Of touching skin and then the parachute
Opening above an old woman asleep
Beside her running shoes—

Snake remembers the warning
Of swaying elephants calling all at once
In the thickening of zoos to the wild ones
At the edge of a blackened field lifting
Orangutans from burn piles—she

Remembers all the animals joined
Together at the edge of twilight whispering
To the rising moon songs of the beauty
Of a world that's gone—

Then bombs in the air—the earth
Dismantled—heavy gas beneath the leaves—
The trees falling—the birds no longer
Calling—never to hear the songs
Of birds again.

The Despot

The severed hand of the despot
Is at first considered an anomaly drawing
Tourists to the new country
Now controlled by the people
Formerly oppressed by that hand.

No one knows what happened
To the body but everyone is grateful
Most of the despot is gone.

Sometimes the hand pinches
Young girls in elevators or in market
Stalls and there is no one to slap
Because the hand moves as a hummingbird
Which was the Aztec god of war.

The people formerly oppressed
Have very little money because their land
Was owned by foreign powers
That held the despot in place
As securely as a nail might hold
A prophet to a beam.

The people raised funds for schools
And hospitals that vanished under
The despot by selling tickets to tourists
Who paid to see the severed hand
Rattling the bars of its cage or scratching
A phantom itch or swatting
A non-existent fly.

In an otherwise empty room
At a rickety card table watched
Through one-way glass by the brothers
And sister of the new government
The severed hand of the despot taps the ash
From a cigarette on the floor—

Drums the table with its thumb
Before picking up the pen to sign
The documents of surrender.

Only then did we hear the sound
Of his other hand clapping.

The Old Man Who Ate Children

There was a bristly old thicket
Inside the oak forests between
School and home snake walked
On her journey between variations
Of corporeal punishment.

In winter when the leaves
Fell you could see tiny birds
Nesting in the white hairs
Of an old man in there who everyone
Said would eat a child.

Snake loved children—in
And outside of her so she wondered
What she could do—

One day with the wind
Tearing acorns off the oaks she
Saw him crying—the birds all
Around him flying—the wind through
The branches dying into stillness

As she crawled to the old man
And fed him her fingers one at a time.

False Positive

I will take from every incarnation
Fire from the mountains—blood from the trees—
Silence from the stones—joy
From rivers—fearlessness from birds
And all of these from your love.

Snake wants to detach her mind
From the processes of death
So she lays down beneath snow-capped
Mountains to the unoiled sound
Of ravens circling the blue petals
Of the wild columbine.

Soul is a coy dervish dancing
Closer then away from death—a breath
Lost on the wind but still there
Moving curtains behind the inward eye
Of an outward glance—a dancing
Tumult blowing through the passes
Of towering victories and doubts—
Moving the seasonal grasses
Enough to drop their seeds.

Please don't worry my dear
Useful slowly disappearing mind—

We will always remember—no
Matter how far apart—

The color of the columbine.

Talking Stick

When the world
Disappears under your feet
Are you falling or
Flying?

The crow will
Say one
Thing

The fox another

And both are
Right.

In Mountains

When snake was physical
She ventured to extreme places
Where the planet ejaculated souls
Out as smoke smothering towns
And fortifying the local belief
That people are livestock
For carnivorous gods.

She wandered the wastelands
Of the prophets where every sunset
Sent a messenger with no eyes
Implying the torch of liberty is
A beacon for the blind—snake

Crawls through snow on her hot
Face sliding downhill into rivers
That carry her out to sea where
She sinks to the bottom only

To find out her ghost can't swim
And that as always it's up to her
To save it or let it drown again.

Chorus

❧

A dark locomotive roars out
Of a mortal wound leaving the warrior
Breathless on the killing field—
Reveling in the blood clotting on blades
Of grass—all that's lost hers—all of it fertilizer
For the poppies that offer
It back to the sun.

Nothing is written—no editors
Work through the night on deadlines
To amend the gesture of a child
Lifting its face to the moon—feeling
The old howls bubble into words—

The answers lie on both sides
Of any point of view—smoking
Like engine fires inside a man running
Down a back road from the laughter
Of his soul bug-eyed in a ditch.

The corn maze is for mystics
Trying to get home—wandering through
Abundance while beset by crows

Who survive by eating the mantras
From the lips of sacred figurines.

After the storm one feather drifts
In an empty sky and if that isn't the edge of
The unknown then why do roses guzzle
Acid rain like retrievers bringing
To the hand an oozing bird.

The mountains rubbed
By wind—the pebbles polished
By rivers—the chorus of leaves
Landing with a thump or the bass
Line of a pumping fist—maybe even
The fingertips erasing sorrow one tear
At a time from the apprentice who transplants
The first into the final hour—

Buildings fall even in this poem—
Maybe in yours as well—snake sees people
Sifting down through an hourglass
Into a future where children are
Pushed out the windows of schools
Using one another for a parachute.

The spirit that has nowhere
To go is ours—it remains no matter
The roadside bomb in the fascist stare

Or the congregations combing anger
From the crust around a beard.

The spirit flits between bodies
In a journey through disappearing doors
At the end of breath—somehow the
Next moment is an artist dipping
Her brush into the lit end of a cigar
Then rendering a single calligraphic
Image of the chosen few on fire.

Sapphires turn blue in the dark
To excite the cravings of thieves
Opening vaults with a notional penis
To withdraw funds to purchase elders
Downstream of a cobalt mine.

Today the malicious prostrations
Before variations of an abacus remain as fresh
And deadly in the airless crypt
Of the untethered mind as the ink
On the blueprints describing how
To genetically modify intolerance
So it will outlive its acolytes.

Something was just injured.
At the edge where consciousness
Provides the refineries to inflame

The spoken word so it's possible
To pretend a cry for help is just
A trumpet blown by wind.

Perhaps we see the victims fade
From view but don't hear them until
We pollinate their open flowers—

Here in the mirage the spilled
Blood of a historic moment—which is
Every moment—gathers in puddles
Thirsty horses drink as an antidote
For cruelties undergone in harness—

Maybe it's not courage
But duty that requires plants to
Stare at the sun until
They're blind enough to bloom—

Or maybe it's the grandmothers
Looking into a river so downstream
Their reflections come ashore to
Ease the sufferings of a child.

If one of us falls out of line
The parade collapses—the horizon

Stops moving away and suddenly—
This is so true—all the dead

Escape the living to become forests
Where extinct birds begin to sing.

This may sound like the chorus
Avoiding what's really happening
By lighting abstractions to smudge
The parlor prior to the séance but

What if all at once we forgave
Ourselves in time to free the brightly
Colored butterflies trapped in the hammer
Descending on this bended nail.

Gardeners spray a white rose
Beneath the window where grandfather's
Snoring awakens grandmother from
Dreaming an heirloom transplanted

From the past refuses to bloom
In a future where we live in hospitals
Exchanging fugue states while sharing
Medicines for surviving the execution
Of one thought by another and another

Which is no different than
Tossing parts of once living creatures
Out the window to pariah dogs.

One only needs to open the trap
Beneath the sink then gargle
What's there—or walk the perimeter
At night chanting—the birdbath is a lake
Where gorgons wash their hair—
To understand death is not afraid
Of us nor is it angry—

it watches as we run away
Or toward it—shuffling in thin gowns
Slit up the back with our asses
Hanging out or sitting on the lap

Of the bombardier as cities
Clarify pink in a scope—

It's with us in rooms when carbon
Monoxide cuts the strings on its guitar—

It attends in alleys
Beneath buzzing neon signs
Helping to tie off a vein—no—
Death is not afraid of us.

It follows the footsteps erased
As they appear—watches the sun—

Puzzled even after so much
Time to think it through why light—
By some incomprehensible law—
Shines without judgement
Equally on us all.

Last One Left

Once there were hot blue waves—the
Two of her asleep in the sand—inseparable—
They lived in agreement everywhere
Inside the endless country of one body—

Ate grapes fresh from the vine—lips
Glossy with squealing light and a shared
Adoration for matching pajamas—

Now snake's lost inside an afterlife—her
Other self is gone—her tongue engaged in licking
The unassembled poem inside of silence—

Waiting for the first kiss of tomorrow
When she steps out of bones to whisper
The lessons learned by wandering between
The regrets of dreamers underground.

The goodness in us never dies.
It sloshes in a bucket halfway up an empty well.

It's not water that drives our thirst—it's
The bucket—the hope someone will drink from us.

Heart Attack

Snake has her infinite tube—
One end stuck in a hospital bed—the
Other in the throat of a ghost loading
Moonlight one beam at a time
Into a catapult aimed at an army

Of remnant voices that don't care
Whose bodies they use to build
A scaffold for their song.

Leadership

If everyone has enough then
Everyone would have enough—

Before the teapot whistles
Manikins break out of store windows
Wearing white shirts with red hats—
Shambling down main street
Trailing dirt like a shovel—

This is the uniform of the old
Guard proclaiming themselves
Immune to the tallyman's
Greasy fingernail—hah—

Snake dances around a burning
Limousine with cigars poking out
The windows waiting for a light.

Hold On

I can't tell you why but all
At once in the attic an old chest
Opens and the yellow pages of a
Diary start crying—alligator tears
Of course—I take it back—I can tell
You why—our personal entries
In the book of sorrow are real
And not meant to fill thimbles
Of grief with gallons of pain.

Hot lips—cold fingers—
Warm touch—snake forgets to be grateful
For times when alongside
The cattle egret she greeted
Each sunrise with the words—
"I've got your back."

Even now inside the cacophony
Of the conductor's wand she wonders
If she was always this afraid—of what
Got lost and what she wore and so
Shouts out—shit—I've been here before.

Original Grace

The lambs are killed early
This year—we need the mother's
Milk and besides their flesh
Is more tender that young.

Drought changes everything—
Hardship knows no gender or age
And my sister who loves women—who used to be
The sad one—is now the happiest
Person in the family because
Even as everything dries up
And blows away she is still there
Inside herself whereas most of us
Though visible are gone.

But the milk is so small
And we need it more than
The ewes who when they get too
Old to have babies will
Go to the circle of red earth
Between doorways and be done
In a flash of knives that catch
Sunlight like shaving glass traps
Angry eyes behind a beard—

Or the way between doors
A story falls from someone's ear—
Becomes a locust creaking
And throbbing in a dead tree—

Little ones to him belong
The man sings in the afternoon heat
With families gathered around
To listen—knowing the words but
Not believing them unless *him* is the man
In the red circle with daughters—

The preacher is a pale man
In a light blue suit who comes
Once a month—he is trained
To preach to us in a church far from
Here where he says they waste clean
Water on bended heads—

He is a strange flightless bird
Gurgling raw noises in his throat—
We are drought-stricken and so
Understand these meaningless sounds
Are prayers for more than rain.

My sister and I try to sing like *him*.
She is beautiful in a purple dress—
Her face like a night sky filled
With moonlit cranes as she gets one word
Exactly right and sings it
Over and over in the language
Of a bucket of dust in a well—
Grace—grace—grace.

Then strange creatures not seen
Except in stories come out of the sky
With wisps of the grandfather's
Beards in their beaks and decorate
The songs of the shaved man
Until he too presumes to correct
Us—teaching us over and over
How to chew the words in our mouth
So they taste like his.

And whatever remains in a bowl
He steals while he sings—he sings
While he steals—he lies while
He sings—he sings while he lies—
Hallelujah he sings—*him* has come
And looking into the dry rivers
We see only the quick black
Snake dragging away pieces

Of vanished daughters
And we know *him* has come—

Him has come we sing
As the blood of the lamb
Mingles with the red dirt
Between our toes—

As the bleat of the lamb
Mingles with the songs of birds
And the songs of praise—

As the daughters disappear
As children into the streets
And return old women ready to die
And the blood of devotion
Drips from ecstasy—word by
Each red word

And at night it is possible
To believe—holding one another
So tightly my sister's skin becomes
Mine as we stand up in one body
To touch the universe
Through the hole in the roof

Deep inside relived to announce
That *him*—hallelujah—is gone.

IMPULSE

Oh how it feels to awaken
On some twilit evening to
A sky throbbing with ravens
And the dry clack of lightening bugs
By whose tiny glow snake sees
Exhausted medics dragging

Soldiers on litters like orphans
Pursued by their skeletons across frozen
Field to an empty house.

Children flit through prisms
Into ever darkening adults—
Evaporating in time—swinging
Lanterns' bright future light at the train
Only they see coming—

Meanwhile snake is vigilant—
Still a child inside a flower with pollen
In her eyes—with bees in her mouth—

Wrapped in a battle flag painted
With images from the lost and found—

Stiff with the blood of everything—
The last drop of the last thing—the

Sumatran rhino twisting against its cage
Decomposed against the bars

As a trampled purse in the stairwell
Of a tower burning down.

BY STORM

Across the drenched countryside
Lightning ripples in white forks
Through personally private purple sky
While bitterns in cold shadows
Boom inside drift logs—between
The murmur of a rising tide receding
Voices cry for more of this.

The last night of the soul is a chandelier
Swaying in a dark ballroom—snake
All grown old and stiff—the crystals
Tingling with captured light inside
The windows of their ancient eyes
While waves lift high enough to drown
The moon inside each diadem.

Snake once danced in that room
With the beloved in her arms—
The sweat running down my sides—
The music growing louder
As we swayed and twirled and pushed
A giant rock up a hill that like
This body was immensely heavy
And not really there.

Unfed

In the middle of the revolution
We set up tables in the streets
And served Thanksgiving dinner
To people with great hunger
But no mouths—people already fading like film inside
Pawned cameras—faces blowing through
A valley of thorns gnawed by thin
Horses following a shrinking river
Away from consciousness.

Red-eyed and charged with electric
Current we thanked each other for liberating
The laboratory rats trapped in the promises
Of leaders—we rearranged their words
With tweezers into laxatives for the generals
Stoppered by fear and ignorance.

We sat alone together—thoughts burning
Down to the fuse—fingered by myths
No one believes anymore as the dead
Recede along a narrow beam while

The few we still remember beckon
Like rainbows in the dark.

Snake into Ploughshares

Snake lived so many
Times she forgot the distraction
Of flesh the way tourists
In an ancient car in a foreign land
Forget the broken springs when
Soldiers point guns at them.

As if we are nothing more than
Broken eggs from which the child
Of something old hatched out—

Snake lived on—with the disquieting
Sensation known to jungle trees
Strangled by orchids that produce
Pungent white flowers monkeys
Use to festoon a nest.

If anyone complains there's no time
To stop the ghost on the other side of the hospital wall
From sucking on bandages in an attempt
To revive its missing heart let them consider
The surgeons pushing back a lock of hair
While blowing beef inside their masks—
Or one of us soaking a handkerchief
In tears from eyes forever pasted to
The image of unlocking the bathroom door

Expecting to find father only to find
An arrangement of red ribbons left
By both barrels of Deus ex Machina—

Or this abandoned factory—where poor
Families sleep forever around a briquette flame until
Authorities investigate vultures
Breaking windows—

Reckoning will come in the form
Of whales stranded in trees—the sacred
Tenderized by mallets in its wound—

Reckoning will be more than a cry
For help lowered by rope halfway down
A mine shaft pretending not to be
A suppository for a scream—

The equations on the chalkboard
Are complex but add up to zero

If subtracted from dreams that oppose
One another—as all dreams do.

With sufficient persistence and
Voluminous hours it's possible to
Create a new calculus where stardust
Turns into cheese or lingerie or death row

Concrete leaking moisture toward a drain
Clogged by hair—anything can happen
When the nursery is unprotected—

The homestead sizzles in the dusky
Red twilight—or is it dawn that staggers
Into sight—like smoke inside the clarinet
When the player exhales an organ through the reed—
Or is it wind inside a thistle seed—

The way in and out is through the door—
On which side of your body do you stand?
Or are you undecided and afraid of that
Shadow disappearing on the floor.

In either case—the bloody
Spear of the charioteer drips with what's
Left of the emperor's sneer.

If only we didn't see so imperfectly—
Our prophets sprout wings to dive
Bomb the little cloister of swallows
Huddled in the bell tower waiting
For the damn bell to stop ringing—

Then Kassandra might come down
The mountain unbuttoning her lips
Instead of her blouse.

(it is not quite a lie to say
Apollo spit in her mouth
But it was snake under her tongue
Whispering the details of future events
That turned her into a seer whom
No one believed—there were feathers on snake's
Tongue but it's not clear if they came from
Swallowing birds or vintage hats—

Or if the truth itself molted
While spelunking in a liar's throat)

In just such a moral wasteland—
With burning tires and salty
Tears on a doll's clicking eyes—

Snake's memory fades from the red
Streaks on El Toro to the illegible
Warning sign at the end of a pier—

It's something not quite the jitter
Of saxophones in a thicket
Among watchful birds—nor even
Lumps of coal squeezed between
Degrees of hate into rapture
In just such a way that a broken
Girl becomes a centerfold.

What snake forgets
Is the dead volcano circled by empaths
Holding hands while chanting
To the angel burning underground
To come end this shivering.

In this necropolis storms
Come from above and leave rain
Water in small depressions left by the knees
Of worshippers waiting for a golden
Voice to come out of the lichen-covered
Hole in the ruined temple where Pandemonium
Shreds curses into sacred thoughts—

It's clear there will come an end
To all things long enough for them
To come again—but through which door—
In the sky—through the temple—or
From the press of moldy battle flags—

Snake hears leaves crackling
Each time she breathes—

She shoves love letters into
The wood stove to warm her premonition
That the radioactive half-life of past
Affections will curl up the chimney
To become a trenching tool
In the hands of an oil minister

Burying his oldest bride while
Sucking her grandmother from the ground.

Before the next verse the world
May resume its spasms wherein one skin
Longs to be inside another so strongly
It consumes everything including
Ragweed—jock straps and barn owls to join
The dance of creation—the frenzy
Of nothing—of nonsense—of wordless
Silence pressing onomatopoeias through
Cell walls to make a baby's cry

Into coherent speech—or primal sound—
Or enchanted stories forged by failure into
The armor of an imbecilic king

While we are left to conclude
Some cat slobbered on our reed—
Hosing each note off a cliff

Below which weary disciples reassemble
The acoustics of a broken heart.

This part of the story is sorted
From broken mirrors in which

A dinghy without oars floats beneath
A blue sky rowed by an enemy's child

Chanting spells at the hole
In the boat filling with water—oh yes—
Partial mirrors are complete mirrors—
And can be a reservoir where
Like a cat with a crusty tail the effete
Lick the bullion off their feet.

Meanwhile the child swims ashore
In time to be adopted by wolves
Who give it the name—wolf—then baptize
It in the river irrigating equally
Tenderness and power.

The next revolution forms behind
The veil of a woman watching men with forked
Beards and bloody fingernails break
Raw eggs into a bowl—

She knows she is the object
Of their lust and scorn—knows
Her death won't inoculate children
From the germs of prophecy—even still

She punches the cleric in the place
Where his sins are snoozing.

Anyone who struggles
To rip off the labels pasted on
At birth—or stands outside watching
Generals pulling capons apart
With their false teeth while
Toasting the harvest moon through
Bulletproof glass—

For that matter—anyone at all—

Knows the cost of riding the truth
Side-saddle into a school for dressage
Is worth the punishment inflicted
For reconfiguring your equipage.

It's the ordinary desires of ordinary
Things—a spigot frozen above a trough
In moonlight with thirsty creatures
Slamming the ice hoping to score
A drink of winter—perhaps it's not that—

But a dunking ordained by preachers
Up to their waist in cold green rivers
Waterboarding an unnamed child—or—

More likely—a single almond sucking one
Hundred gallons of rain from the hookah in the ground.

This citizen stepped out of the crowd
In perfect health—this one crawled through filth
With eyes closed—its mouth filled with
Croquet balls and cheese—both siphon the feverish
Warmth from a burning recliner then leave
Everything in a bequest written in plastic
To the offspring of endangered whales—
This is how books get written
By those who create historic events
While driving an ambulance over a cliff—
Or how each author learns to breathe
Submerged beneath the empty page—

Even so—the impulse to leave everything
Behind—to look away from the smoke
Drifting off the burning bride—

Mimics the heartbeat inside a gold coin
In the wishing well of a narcissist
Fornicating with lost principles.

This is the end of a long migration
In which the birds of the world

Travel everywhere in an attempt
To stitch the planet back together—

Into one vast quilt depicting
The meteor that strikes the last
Yogi asleep on hot coals who then
Stretches to touch all living things
With the magic wand in his drawers—

The imbeciles wrap each other's
Parachute while escaping through a fog
Of pepper spray—they leave welts
On the electorate that blind generals
Touch like melon testers to foretell
The moment youth ripens enough
To store inside the pantry of a flag—

But enough—seasons change—the apples
In the mirror are ready to pick but the trees
Where they hang leave no reflection—

Only this dangling silence—the
Orchard is honored for the same
Reason we admire the shaman who called
Down from the sky enough rain
To clean a bandage for reuse.

For the kings and the generals
This is a walk between crosses—

A turning away from the harvester
Whose shiny blades catch light
Before slicing the silence into
Infinite pieces each one of which
Is codependent on a gun.

Snake exudes the past—former
Inklings turn to reflexes piped through
Muscles into ripples on a black pond
Overhung by unformed futures waiting
For the moment when the human face
Rises out of the water like a flashlight
Illuminating the periphery
Of the unknown beyond which targets
Are groomed to be expendable.

We are here only right now—
Trembling in each other's arms—

Incidentally atrocious as mimes
Shoveling mimes out of silence
Into a furnace fueled by words—

Let us go then—into the fire
To save our voice before it burns.

Vistas

The boulevards were loud
With war engines rumbling into cities.
"Sgt. Pepper" was the soundtrack
Scraped from hobnail boots. The
Traffic light means nothing to a tank.

A socially acceptable policy
Regarding the complete destruction
Of witnesses was arranged between
Triggers and fingers planning to load
Everything into the secular mouth
Of ministers whose words shot flaming
Prophets from carnival guns.

Once snake entered a train station
Where men walked each other like
Dogs walking dogs—timing their watches
So as not to miss the locomotive
Of abundance paid to pick them up—

They hurried past the vestibule
Where suffragettes burned ballots inside
Frozen voting booths to keep warm.

Somewhere a penis is lecturing
Its owner about the right way to defile
A manikin and leave no seminal trace
Of its criminal regard—soon schools
Will form around these stories—generations

Will believe in them as they set forth
To colonize a mushroom cloud.

Used Cars

Snake gets a full tank of gas, fresh
Wash and wax job—clean
Seats, GPS on the dash—
Spare in the trunk—sign on
The dotted line—drive it away—

Snake don't remember doin
This but must have because here
She is—on the road—cruisin—
Checkin directions once in awhile
But mostly just flyin by the seat
Of her tail—down the highway—cities—
Towns—deserts—forests—friends—
Enemies—strangers—got horses
Running in a field and her little spotted dog
Curled beside her—warm as a baked
Potato where they touch—

Car's dusty and dirty—got stains
On the armrest—radio don't work
So well—tires low and bald—runnin
On empty—don't look nothing like when
Snake picked it up so long ago—

She drives to another lot—turns
In the clunker—gets another one—motors on—
Likin the clean upholstery—sure—she's
Forgotten everything about that old

Car except—sometimes in her dreams—
The warm body of the little dog.

Chorus

There's werewolves and vampires
Shambling up next to me sliding
And hiding from the light
Bouncing off the stone and still despite
Their company I feel alone
Until a block away a trumpet groans
Out some blue mist I breathe
In like a hit of good weed and by
And by I get a musical contact
High and bringing my phantoms
With me step into this stairway
Leading down to the red door where
The jazz pours out like rivers
Between afterlives.

No one is safe when the waves of sound
In the air flare up the stairs like honey
Through jubilation bees and right
Then my plans for the evening unravel.

My friends save me from going
All tenor sax and unfiltered cigarettes
By shaking the powdered E-flats
Off my hat and leading me to a dump
That serves wine in paper cups.
I'm fine with this moment until
The barmaid comes up and pours
Her face all over mine then twitches
Her nose until my nose itches
And I say sons of bitches to the beauty
All around me I can't see

While she swishes into the dark
Corner of the bar where nothing moves
Except shadows and the remains
Of other days and other
Ways of being alive than this.

The jazz is everywhere and yeah
I love the city and its cold heart
And lack of pity for the broken apart
When someone jumps through a window to get
Where they wanna go but man I'm scared
In a three-pack-a-day way that I'll never touch the sun
Or hear real coyotes howl again.

The Elephant in the Room

It's only come here because
The rivers are dry or undrinkable—
Silted over with sand—the acacias—
Some thousands of years old—dead—
Their leaves torn off by storms
The way soldiers fieldstrip cigarettes.

The elephant is in the room
Because now it must raise
Its young among our furniture
And on our carpets and sure it might
Break a vase or punch
Out a window or drink with
Its delicate pink nose
From the toilet bowl but please
Don't chase it away.

The days of walled-off
Abundance and personal
Habitat are over.

ADOPTING

The child snake never birthed sits
At the end of her bed as she sleeps—
Asking why no one made space
For her and the answers all
Seem hollow and disproportionate
To the size of the mountain
She climbed to come here.

I tell her I had my own life
To live and she tells me she was my
Life—unclaimed as the one
Mitten in the lost and found.

She tells me of her brothers
And sisters and millions of animals
In her world that no one wants
And how they time-travel between
Love and hate—between distance
And closeness as if strung with wire
On a necklace in the dark.

So now my ghostly daughter
How do we proceed through these
Years apart—before we stand side

By side in the warm familiar
Cauldron of a star mingling our light

Like melted bears holding
Each other in the limbs
Of a burning tree.

OUROBOROS

When the breath ends
The journey begins—
Where the journey ends
The dream begins—
When the dream ends
The breath begins—
When the breath ends
The journey begins—

Snake is empty and full.
Empty of herself—full
Of herself—and by the friction
Between these great disorders
The spark is formed—

Momentarily lighting the room
Where we untie the noose around one
Another's neck with the same
Hands that put it there.

VISION

Snake watches the still tide—
Empty of life—clear quiet water
Reflecting sky—fragments of light—
Nothing but water and sky
Until she moves closer and sees
Her reflection—hisses at that nasty
Thing—don't like it—be out of focus—
Eyesight must be failing—inexplicable
Goblin hosing down her mind—

Snake moves further and deeper through
The endless years of solitude—she sees
Crumbled towers—got shadows pimping
Bones to hang a living body on—
Got the residue of thoughts
Flitting outside demented minds that once
Sheltered them—she crawls toward

A face that always moves away—
Understands this is her face—our
Face—as the scattered parts

Of things let go of the energy that
Binds them—she's turning
To mist—into the imaginary number
In a theorem that proves nothing can
Be understood until the ladder leading
Out of this illusion is returned
By those who got away.

BIG TEMPORARY

Now that snake be eternal
He understands all them previous
Measurements used to express
Variation on the idea of time
Be like slapping a bow tie
On a scarecrow—pretty soon
Tie's gone—crop's eaten and big
Temporary's guarding the field.

Time be a granular cat—
Like Mr. Sandman—

Snake looks for residue
Of last days as she slithers through
The feathers and peels—pork rinds
Of yesterday—looks for her
House—her little dog—her wife—

Digs through endless layers—
Finds teeth in asphalt pudding—
Streaks of gold with fingernails—
Pumice held in place by hair—
Digs into the body of earth—into
Armpits and pubic bones and clavicles

Of iron and clay—finds a mirror—
Cleans it—sees the old world exactly
As it used to be stand up
And shake out its frightful hair.

Sees willows along the banks
Of rivers with horses floating by—sees
Signs held by students in front
Of men with guns—silhouettes of women
Bearing children aloft like candles
As they march toward fire—sees
Blood on gift wrapping—sees everything
In the mirror disappear again—

Then her dead child looks
Out at her across the distance
Both infinitely near and far—

Not even the speed of light is fast
Enough to measure how quickly
Love turns over the hourglass
When we meet again.

Odd Duck

Snake hides in the outhouse behind
The homestead while end-of-the-world
Gangs move through rooms in search of food—
Eatin shreds of yellow lace—lickin da cat box brah—
Gnawin underarms off old shirts for salt—

She hears furniture splinter inside
The house—hears the cursin
Barefoot things usin both hands to break
Windows—cuttin their knees suckin residual
Taste of sunset from the glass—

The smell of honeysuckle growin
Over the outhouse fails to overcome
The ancient vapors trapped inside
The pew where generations of homespun
Gods were discommoded—debatin the merits
Of prayers squeezed out of tenderloins—

Snake remains inside a companionable
Discomfort to care for the doves whose
Only way out of the human heart
Is through a burning door.

STRAIGHT JACKET

The valley and hills
Of this empty planet were named
For prophets who electrified
The fences around followers
With stern commandments
Expunged from addled minds
Like lice from dirty snoods—

Now that nothing of anything
Is left these hills echo with the songs
Of rivers spanning geologic time—rain into
Rivulets becoming streams that run
To the sea dancing and singing without fear
Of retardants—dams or toxic spills.

Snake lives on the corner of mumbo
And jumbo—as the sole occupant she spends
Days in a box wrapped in magnets
Hiding from robots made of steel—

It's her bad fortune to escape the asylum
Only to be chased by doctors who think
Transplanting compassion between bodies is
A matter of removing the circuit breakers
That connect a promise to a lie.

Gone

Waves tumble out of nonexistence
Into living forms with the excitement
Of huskies pulling an empty sled
Across a crust of yellow snow—

Snake begins to pinch the slow
Fester of time from the wounds
In her tail—expelling birds, trees,
The smoky honey inside stories—oysters—tarts
With rouged faces—pimps with pompadours—
Tentative and fragile—awakened

Blind at first as last—

The metaphor is dying—the truth
Which is eternal when left to itself
But variable in the minds of the living
Feels the sag of meat on bones—

Feels bodies renewed—universe groaning
With laughter and songs and suffering
And flowers seeking in the dark planet
The iron rain that powers the
Soloists in their bloom—

The past—present—and future—
Coming again—surrounding the innocent
And the guilty and those

Walking out of personal darkness
Tossing matches to briefly illuminate
A world made of paper.

LEARNING TO BREATHE

A quark stumbles out of a collider
Into a vast ballroom where a shy atom
Sits in a darkened chair until asked
To dance—gravity plays a tango to which
The unimaginable whirls the impossible
Into a creature that steps up to the microphone
To sing in a language only the mermaids

Tangled in plastic inside a choking whale
Understand actually describes the depth
Of the canyon beneath the surface of a loving
Touch and the exact moment when

Yesterday's child is reborn.

The Border Shift

Snake hands her pistol butt-first
To the officer but at the last second
Revolves it quickly backward
Then flips it half a turn sideways
So that it's now pointed
At the authority impersonator
Looking for illegal souls.

It's tempting to pull the trigger
And be done with it—to kill
All mythological devils then hightail it into
The desert where snake is at home
With other not-always-real snakes.

Every story is dangerous.
Even the truth has a rough crossing
When it's voiced—the moral or lack of it
A wandering prospector dying
Of thirst all alone with a fortune
In gold on her back—

Let the story live—let the listener
Decide if it's true—some will believe
It and some won't but it is the only
Possession of the one who earned
The right to tell it
By counting the pulse
Of a rose with one hand
And with the other winding a clock
That ticks inside a velvet bomb

So soft it inflicts no more pain
Than dying in a dream—

One day we will make
The authorities answer
For what they did and didn't do
And we will publicly paddle
The ones whose insufficiencies
Breached from their mouths
Like dolphins from a fascist's eye—

They'll answer for the shadows
Layered over the poor creatures
Seeking refuge in our hearts—

That day is coming—soon—
When this hell finally freezes over.

Chorus

The children cried
The children threatened
The children screamed
No one listened

The adults put a foot down
Something got squished
They put the other one down
And called this living

The children pointed
The children said it's gone

The adult asked where it went

And the children cried
The children threatened
The children screamed
No one listened

Healing

Before mother earth got sick people
Got sick—snake remembers the world
Abandoning men and women as they
Awakened to blood on their pillows
And hands tied behind their backs—

Earth shook free of everything—from
Limes and coral and ears of corn—closing
The door behind her to the fuse burning
Down to the keg—then the big boom
When folks got numb inside—

Sick bodies—arthritic—inflamed—
Taken by cancer—doctors treating one disease
With another called chemotherapy.

Snake knows that word holds
The blessing—the remedy—
The antidote—

Right there—
In the middle—

mo—ther—
"Mother."

GIBLET GRAVY

Start with a world—pared into
Pieces—bits of folks—some botanicals—
Maybe some donkeys and a possum
Or two—don't forget the fur and hair
And lips and stems and parings
From the manicure booth—

Throw in some storm drain
Algae—some dead sea scroll—maybe
Pollen from a pharaoh's tomb—
Remember the beaks and fingers—
Snouts and stems—when you sit down
At the devil's table bring a
Long fork and a short reach.

Simmer this but don't boil it—
Warm it enough to thicken
In a broth—stir it so it don't
Stick—taste it with a finger—

War thinks snake—it tastes like war—
When the brain climbs down the spine
To stop the hand reaching
Out to comfort a stranger.

Hip Cat

Snake learns it takes more than one
Lifetime with a spindle to weave blood
And hair back into something whole
That was broken by degrees—

There's borders everywhere—
Distance between things asleep
In the same tree—take one step
And you're on somebody's foot—
Stay where you are and wake
Up at the wheel of a tractor
Pulling a soul out of a corpse—

Time to push back thinks snake.
Time for disbelieving the illegible
Fortune inside the stale wafer
Shared between fetish and faith—

So snake stays warm in the glow
Of steam rising from the instigators
Whose hiding places are too small
To cover the enormity of their crimes
And whose days are numbered.

EYES OPEN

Out in the wheat stubble horses
Walk slowly away from the alien
Crumbling its parachute
Into a small ball before eating
It until there's nothing left
But the alien—the wheat stubble—and
The horses running from riders
They refuse to carry.

It's been about a thousand years
Since the last ship hovered above
A cluster of stone pyramids helping
People washing clothes and babies
In a muscular blue river unspool a civilization
Out of confessions extracted from shrieks
Diluted with white wine then sold
As an aphrodisiac to the ruling class—

Snake settles between the golden
Stalks taking the time to whisper
Down into next year's roots the ancient
Promise of a new beginning
That tastes so sweet when spread
On bread but bitter when served
At the point of a sword.
Forgiveness liquefied into tears
Flows downstream—yes—but upstream
As well in the rivers of melted hours

Where grandmothers hang diapers
On a thorn bush in the sun.

Snake rests like we rest—in
Herself—but always awake—afraid
To close her eyes because
Out in the wheat something shiny
With a feral edge of madness
Is composing elegies to future
Children forced to carry stones

Up the hill to build a monument
To the next abandonment—

Whose bellies form autumn flowers
As they lift the weight
Their parents couldn't budge.

Country Learning

When snake was a little feller
In striped overalls draggin a can
By a string on the way to school—
Wearin her brother's outgrown boots
On feet been bare all summer—

She watched how birds
Move together as they fly—how they
Yield without touching yet
Are one bird to the sky.

She tries to live like that—be
Exactly the thing she is but at peace
With everything she's not—wide enough
To harness a plow with pappy but narrow
Enough to skip rope with friends.

Milk the cow—suck on grass—
Help collect brown eggs at dusk—

Snake moves toward a future
Silent as a solar-powered voice
Waiting for daylight to sing.

Echo

❧

The words are rough pebbles
Worn smooth by fast talkers—over
And over until they mean nothing
To anyone not already deafened
By the ocean in a blue suit
Retching up clustered straws—

Choking on the trash leavening
The air when insincerity becomes
The engine that may incidentally throw
Tears out the window of an eye—

Meaningless words gargled like gasoline
Way back in the turbine of a lie
Can't power compassion into action

Which is why the roadside
Attractions between kindness and touch
Sells screams inside of bottles.

In the opalescence of an empty shell
Shines the halos of fallen angels—

Who got so close to the living—who
Slept in the bodies of their charges
Like customers leaving porn shops
Slipping on their wedding ring—

They discovered that one lifetime—
No matter how brief or lit with pain—
Is better than infinities of servitude
To gods that smell of cutting boards.

And so the angels spread
Their beautiful tears inside the pink
Shells the next tide takes
Out to salt the sea.

The past is a decaying pile
Of names and places within
Which our current identity moves
Like worms through compost.

In back alleys a blanket
That once draped a favorite
Chair in front of a television
Set where the financial news
Blares twenty-four hours a day passes
Between shivering bodies
Until it is worn so thin it can't
Warm a swaddling ghost—

Later a truck driver sees
This blanket lying beside a ditch
And runs over it—

The blanket is actually a belief
Unquestioned for centuries by men
Who leak blood from their smiles while
Leaving tributes along the highway
To a black velvet painting of fox
Around an orphaned fawn.

A migrant comes out of the orchard
With empty hands calling the names
Of his children still high in the trees—

He is just trying to instruct spirits
The proper way to climb down a ladder—

He teaches his children the language
Of love—of labor—of the resins
On the hands when permitted
To touch the fruit of another.

In the cave it was told
Every child is born into sin—
Born nasty—born with the devil
In its heart and life is a journey taken solely
To shake that thing loose—

Born and will die into sin
And in between better be
Regaling the gods with amen.

Snake believed this
Until the first time she died to

Discover she was
From jump street immaculate
And on her own to stay that way.

The ammo dump in the general's
Closet explodes blowing his straightjacket
High enough to block the sun—

Meanwhile Diana waits outside
A pistol range—drinking the thunder
While the winter crows sleep

In the inflammation the gods
Of war harvest from her eyes.

It begins with pinching flesh
To assure we are still alive and not
Just some phantom ogling
The bodice of a gun.

These who profit from death
Worship inside morgues to the thickening
Smoke of candles inside a wound—

Or in jail cells beside open
Drains thanking Hippocrates
For helping tie off reluctant veins.

Light travels its entire lifetime
Which is forever to expose the fingers
Of the bearers of black flags
Who are trapped mid-stride
Between surrender and attack
Like the breath of an old bluesman
Inside a pawned trombone

While in the hedges around
This the moist lips of the gods
Kiss the dead birds until
They bloom dark red in the minds
Of taxidermists trying not to stoke
The fires of lost love.

In the particle collider cruelty
Slams into history thus the weapons
Of war are revealed—grain
By grain of prayer—minute lisp
Of broken vow—splinter of a child's

Last trust—while the witnesses
Are created from the residue
Of not the act but the shadow
Of the act of looking away.

What's not postponed—what's
Not old but was never new surges
Through wires connecting

Rain to thirsty flowers that as
They bloom assure us beauty
Is more than the child of purpose—

And who will distribute
The handwritten notes passed
Between the earth and stars
Suggesting for those alive right now
No sufficiency of good intention
Will make a better yesterday.

There is no other river.
There is no local air.

Seizure

There's still childhood blood
In snake's brain—the doctors
Are amazed she didn't convulse
Sooner—at least she hasn't started—
As one said—playing the piano
With no piano near.

Moyamoya maybe one says—
Like the difference between gill netting
Or long-lining—the brain fishes for oxygen
Any way it can—when the central arteries
Fail lots of little ones come out to catch
The force that keeps poetry alive—

It's the same blood in her head
That a six-year-old carried to school
Like an apple in a lunchbox—

There is no spellcraft here.
If there were this old blood would've
Bled out through a skinned
Knee or scabbed elbow and not clotted
Its wagons around a modern town
Where settlers dying is postponed

Until an ancient locomotive arrives—
Its steam whistle hot and piercing
As an owl crying to the stars before
The branch beneath it breaks.

First Breath

Today we come home—
To this mind—to this body—
In new countries of skin
And bark and fur—home from
Restless dreaming—home
From the taste of black vials
And shattered panes of light—of
Sudden ectoplasmic suns.

Our exile—it is over. Here—
On this land—in this dirt—
We are forgiven.

There are no conclusions
Like boulders altering the flow
Of a river on its way to the sea—

Once a woman stood up inside
Her tattoos offering her heart to the sky—
To the trees—to the song in between—

She will do this again—maybe she's
Doing it now—while everyone is running away.

VISITATION

Snake came across a tiger—
Or its bones—or the fog from its bones—
Or the shadow of its appetite—streak
Of dark eyes blinking in quartz—lost
Chromosomes of yesterday's light—

Oh the tenures of tomorrows
Caged in things—beneath the swollen
River cutting new channels
Around dead willow tiger looks out
Without speaking—this is snake's story—yes—
With tiger in it—but not the same
Tiger watching right now—

What tiger hopes snake
Will say—snake says—her words
Like a gouache painting of a stork lifting
A child from an ocean of blood—

She gathers ice into her tail
Like a feather dipped in ichor to sketch
Exits ramps for lovers disabled
By the enormities of need—

Snow falls everywhere—randomly
Building a snowman that dances when
No one is around—so dance—

Surely by now it's safe to say—
No one is around.

DEVOTION

There's a book open to a picture
Of a demented robot in a cornfield fitting
A prosthesis on its neck as the sun rises golden
Over a tallow pond—not a children's
Book but the colors are so exquisitely rendered
Snake wonders if everything repellent
Isn't just a beautiful ornament stolen
By wolves from the dowry
Of a bride abducted by the sun—

She turns the page on the book
To the story of an old man parking his truck
Beside a sparkling field late at night—

The old man gets out of the truck—
Leaves the keys beside his old dog
Curled up next to its favorite toy—

Everything about this moment is old—
Except the small tail movement
Of the dog which is as new
As a shivering blue arctic flower—

He walks into the field as if entering
A door in another self—each step
Crunching starlight in the frozen grass—
Breathes out—he says it—
Breathes in—he says it—
Breathes out—Now—

Breathes in—Wow—
now—wow—now—wow.

Back in the truck his old dog
Joins in as best she can—
bow—wow—bow—wow.

What It Is

Snake sees Bob Marley lowered
Into a hole in the sand with his ganja
Sticks and Les Paul guitar—she's
In tears—don't matter what's real—
The sheen on her dreads is as
Purple as Rapunzel's dream—

At the back of the crowded
Street right across from the drugstore
Cowboys practice their craft
By pulling each other's zippers down
While the organ grinder's
Monkey picks up the copper
Pennies the mortician left behind—

There's a table in the summer
Orchard where the nuns write manuals
Regarding the efficacy of cattle prods
To instruct children how to pray—

What ripens inside tartare
Constellates in a shot glass
With a lipstick smear on the rim.

In the distance a small
Locomotive works hard up a steep
Grade—dragging everything
From—or into—view—
The sound of its wheels

And the rattling of its body
Opening a window into silence—

Under the ground beside
The rails newborn mice tremble
Like string instruments tuned
To the key of an incoming round.

Meanwhile the coconuts
Float off in the receding tide
As the figure sniffing its
Fingers salvages the colors
Of freedom from the prism
The inkling sun leaves

In the imprints left by the last
Dead thing to walk away.

It's all jambalaya thinks snake—a
Cauldron filled with sensible shoes
And first editions cooked into sunrise
Dribbled on a nursery rhyme.

Rabbit Hole

The promoters neglected
Their toupees and went out bald
Because they were distracted
By the end of intermission.

Here in this iron cage
All the forgotten gods no longer
Attached to any belief
Fight one another with bare knuckles
Until the one left is carried on a stretcher
By the audience to a hospice
Of rubble and flowers where its
Rage lives on forever as scribble
On a desert stone.

It's easy to stop the gods.
Just stop believing they're real.

VILLAGE

The little boy on the stoop is dirty
From wallowing in mud where
Neighbor kids pushed him down—now
He's crying at a door that never
Opens except when someone inside
Brings the prisoners out.

The little boy is actually a little girl
Who is actually a baby bird who is truly
A colt caught in barbwire after
A night of running from fireworks but
Truthfully is anyone afraid the next
Moment might expose a long finger
Poking a precipice closer.

What pulls us apart is also what
Holds us dear to one another
If only we'd see past the simian figure
Crouching under the low ceiling inside
An innocent gaze.

This world is in pieces—we are
The pieces that when fit together narrate how
Broken arrows are still weapons
When used by broken men.

WITHOUT REGRET

Some were excited by death—
Hooking sleds to fatal impulses then
Dragging them north into the ecology
Of an unstrung bow—they were not soldiers—but
Curbside retainers for malevolence
No one thought to empty even when
The Epilobiums died of the smell.

To the whirring sound of cicada
Inspired by cellos in an orchestra
Of ghosts celebrating formlessness
With dirges for the rippling of pain
Through skin—rainbows slammed the planet
With fists of glorious color while thunder
Broke and boomed above the few
Remaining figures willing to unwrap
The child inside a rotten flag.

Cults of violence rose
From trash barrels and couch
Fires—chased by apparatchiks
Through rooms filled with pawn shop
Furniture riddled by pitchforks
And lit by tallow lamps—

The work is to put the fires out
Before the path is burned—or
To start them so it is.

BARTENDER

There's a tavern inside of snake
That never closes—lit with beer
Signs—neon-streaked faces, shadows under
Tables—where it's still legal to smoke—
Brass rail along the bottom of the chestnut
Bar brought from Dublin on a whaler.

George Thorogood walks in—sits
At an empty table—orders one bourbon—
One scotch—one beer.

In a corner Misery adjusts her skirt
Allowing the garters holding up her torn
Stockings to show against a gleaming
Pasture of ghost colored thigh—

Misery picks up her drink—slides
Through the crowd standing
Back to back near the jukebox
Twitching to unearthly music
While slopping drinks on the floor—

Snake watches this in the big mirror
As she counts auras through the haze—

Misery stands in front of Lonesome
George—says hi—mind if I join you—
My name is Misery—and I love company—

George looks up—says—I drink
Alone—with nobody else—you know
When I drink alone—I prefer
To be by myself.

That's how it goes in the bar
That never closes inside the dream
Where snake mixes strange particles
Into flaming glasses in such a manner
That once in a while a customer explodes
Back into a body as it's born.

One Sky

Ever lose something—
Have it come back and then
Remember you forgot to hold
It close when it was yours?

Ever see hope leave the eye
Of strangers crushed by burdens
So large they're fossilized in their pants
While around them harvest
Drips from the sickle of a child?

Extraordinary—ordinary—root
Or blossom—no difference—the irony
Inside the eye like a seam of pure gold discovered
In a miner's grave—secretions of
Lizards dripping from a sacred chant—

Snake looks into her memories
Like a mirror where an emperor is bathed
And rouged by embalmers while his
Old wardrobe blows down the road

Past gangs of children who prefer
Going naked rather than put on
The rags of empire.

Speaker of the House

The baby looks at the bird
On the open windowsill.
Sees the window and the bird.

The old man on the bench
Looks at the pigeons at his feet.
Doesn't see his feet.

Both are hungry for something
But if snake may intrude what they need
Most is to be considered real
By anything other than death.

This is how prophecy begins—by
Looking but not seeing—then

Translating the approximate view
Into doctrines gargled back and forth

From increasingly preposterous stories
That are then folded into fresh diapers
For an incontinent mind.

HIDDEN WATER

So it was the Garamantes
Looked into the sand storm
As shamans look into pelvic
Bowls for portents and saw
The light grow dim in midday
Like an eclipse of the sun turning
The dunes first crimson then ochre
And the first to see this pulled
Their robes over their children
While camels stumbled blindly
Into air thick as meal.

Survivors lifted out of the dust
Like storks from a heat mirage—sat
Around fires after long hours
Gathering what livestock wasn't buried
To the neck or impounded like stakes
Beneath the circling larks—

Gone snake remembers under
A bronze sky with her possessions
On her back—gone—leaving a dry season
From which rain will come one day to
Renew this inhabitable tear.

A Rock and a Hard Place

When the gray fog lifts I'm
Your rescuer waiting on the edge
Of the chalky blue cliff where
Black wave-worn stone projects
Above a beach loud with gulls
Picking apart stranded fish.

The fog is a national treasure in that
It assures collective blindness or at least
A softening of the sounds from a sinking
Boat—filled with refugees from empty
Cities handcuffed to the gunnels—slow
To become visible from shore.

They are too far away to save.
Snake can't swim that far past
The blockade formed by lifeguards
Looking inland to their lovers
Who service tourists by showing
Them how to sharpen innocence into
Something used to open cans.

Someone will surely intervene.
Maybe we are reading a book
About an interrogation in a prison
When suddenly living inmates
Appear at our table drinking
From a cup of broken teeth
In which a tongue calls for freedom.

So we wait throughout
Our days—throughout history—
For the faces the tide brings in
Once the boats go down—and
When the little boy covered
In kelp and crabs finally washes up

On the sand our job is to frighten
The gulls away long enough to place
One gentle vista in his cloudy eyes
So he may feel loved in whatever
Afterlife has him now—

But this won't happen in time
To save him—or his brothers—
Or his sisters—or ourselves.

BOUQUET

Children playing off the trail
Find the buried grenade below the Dendrobiums
Dropping their beautiful yellow flowers from
The canopy of banyans that spill
Old rain on the detritus when wind
Disturbs the upturned leaves.

A little boy ties a vine to the grenade—
Wraps it in yellow petals and moss then
Drags it down the path behind him
On his way home for dinner.

Because snake loves this little boy
And his parents she is happy to report
The grenade did not explode and no
One was killed or maimed this time.

The little boy grows old—forgets
The forest—the ladles of stewed hen
With sunlight spilling across the table—
He travels the world with this grenade

Telling crowds that no one is safe
As long as death is one curious child
Away from the war to end all flowers.

SHORT GOODBYES

Her tail lashins done disturbed
The mountains until landslides
Tumble down exhuming a little feller all dried
Up with bits of wingtips still on his feets—old
Parchment filled with faded writin
Clutched between cracklin
Fingers like an atavistic wing—

Snake respects this thing—don't
Want to disturb its final sleep so covers
It back up but first memorizes the
Words describin the end—

Yes—I closed my eyes—
Father lights a candle—places
It on a paper boat in the current—
We get in and drift away.

Snake the Other

No tricks today she thinks
Watching the jogger through the scrubby
Brush beneath the billboard
Featuring a grinning predator
As traffic zooms past—

Coyote eyes the closest cover
A fast sprint away—by a gas station
That reeks of her ancestors there's
A thicket of blackberries.

She was caught by early sunrise
Coming right behind the full moon
While eating tossed shreds of bun
And burger from a bag—boom—
Suddenly visible and never
Has she been this thoughtless
But man that burger—so
Now let's get out of here.

Brush to thicket to dumpster
To overpass to apartment hedge
Then some time in open
Space dodging the fucking cars
Then through it up the hill
To the tree line overlooking
The highway to her pups.

Death is close—magic is afoot—
She feels it moving through the city

Or sleeping curled beneath
The ghost lights in the sky—magic
Is the open eye falling but never
Landing in what it fears—

Coyote lets her heart—her nose—
Her love for the running start
Lead her paws back home

With some of the burger
Warm in her mouth
For her pups.

Chorus

Who here is ready to turn the other
Cheek so the eyes follow the head
In order to see what's really happening
Beyond the small perch where the mind
Sits in a vibrant arrangement of plastic
Flowers knitting excuses for turning
Out the lights—or—more accurately—
Is the choice to murder nothing
The beginning of grace—

And what of the children standing
Beneath the shadows of monuments—
The patina of events on their upturned
Faces like moss on a cannonball—
Realizing ancestors are the enemy—

We the chorus mention the figures
Eating mushrooms from the black dirt
Of a freshly dug grave but why
Speak of the dead or those who attend
Them when no poem can encompass
The strange beauty of the white lilies
Fading to amber beneath sparrows
That count us as we fall—

The companies who start the fire—
Who sicken into old men by forgetting cost
Is different than value—who hunt in vain
For the trophy sheltering under
A dress to hang it in their heads—
Are now run-off dreams of ashen rain.

A whaling ship lurches past the headlands
As if it were real—boldly asserting its
Presence by running up the pennants
That announce the mirage is breaking free
Of the illusion with enough force to shatter
The spectacles the gorgons wear—

The ship is loaded to the gunwales
With cetacean parts—with bones for hair
Pins—blubber to trace a palimpsest—
Tongues for the songs they sing through
The bunghole when salted into casks—
Everything needed to construct
A good or bad or indifferent passage
Through the cold currents that
Flow between tomorrow and today.

The cargo includes beakers of enzymes
Doled out to the constipated captain
Straining to push out something like—ahoy—
While polishing the hereditary spear
He repeatedly throws at himself—

Who learned the trade winds—the variables
And fatal latitudes from the cook
Who is the only passenger to survive nights
Spent cutting cheese on the captain's Bible—

A ghost who babbles in the tongue
Of a setting sun speaks a language

That reveals the anicent
Enmity between a telescope
And gods who can't be seen

The ship is trapped between centuries
Unaware that it sank—it hovers between dreams
In the place it last remembers
As an acrobat in midair reaches for what
Isn't there—shall we mention the captain
Is finally unbuckling his belt—charts
Confirm the moment has come to release
His pent-up hunger into the sea
Which beyond giving personal relief
Assures the harpooners the whales will surface
Because they cannot breathe—

The ship wanders alone from one
Skin to another—below the waves
Inside the catacombs of liquid grace—

The whales are gone—spread across dry
Land in the bobbins and lamps and buttons
And in forgotten books where they
Still swim among pressed flowers.

There's nothing left but snake
Rocking the boat on the quiet blue sea
Of an emboldened fable watching a damaged
Species sell tickets to its own demise—

And for those in the lifeboat drifting—

Toward one last chance or the two
Hands still reaching above the water—

Each attached to different worlds—
One familiar as the butcher's thumb—the hand
That waves the flag and pounds the drum—

Or the other—unfamiliar to all
But flowers in the morning sun—

Which one will you save?

LOVE AND GRATITUDE FOR THE FRIENDSHIP,
MENTORSHIP AND KINSHIP OF

Roger Lemons
John Huey
Erich Schiffmann
Anne Jablonski
Norman Dubie
Carie Garret
Jenny Van West
Clint Willis
James Lemons
Sharon Doubiago
Anette Berg
Xulia Duran-Rodriguez
W. Nick Hill
Jamie and Michael Foster
Dirk Nelson
Alexis Rhone Fancher
Gregory Jerozal
Christa Pierson
Jennifer Willis
Christine Schmucker

I am also deeply grateful to Red Hen Press and their outstanding staff for the support and trust I've received over the years. Especially the invaluable counsel and contributions made to this book by Kate Gale.

Biographical Note

Original Grace is the fourth book in the *Snake Quartet* and the eighth collection of poetry published by Gary Lemons. Gary worked many jobs, mostly involving hard labor outdoors, to underwrite his life as a poet, but the one dearest to his heart is planting over five hundred thousand trees in the logged-off, high-elevation forests of the Pacific Northwest. He attended the Undergraduate Poetry Workshop at the University of Iowa, where he studied with John Berryman, Donald Justice, Marvin Bell, and Norman Dubie. He now teaches yoga at Tenderpaws Yoga Studio, owned jointly with his wife, Nöle Giulini.